MW00607483

Jane Jamison

Wendy Scheirer

James David Sloane

Harry Dunn

John Suplee

Martin May

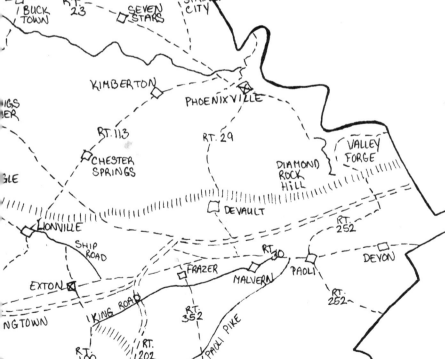

Sandra Giangiulio

Sandra Severson

Sketches By Marc Reed Hamer

THE FOUR SEASONS OF CHESTER COUNTY VOL. IV

About the cover

Chester County artist Richard Bollinger sketches from his canoe the surreal waters and sunrise above Eagle's Marsh Creek Lake as the curtain went up on June 17, 1998.

This is the *604* copy of a limited edition of 3,000 books

THE FOUR SEASONS
Red Hamer
Author And Photographer

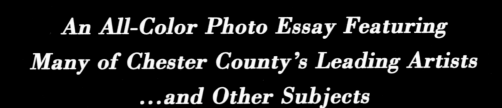

An All-Color Photo Essay Featuring

Many of Chester County's Leading Artists

...and Other Subjects

Published and Distributed By
Four Seasons Book Publishers
Red Hamer, Owner-President
P.O. Box 0222
West Chester, Pa. 19381

Copyright © 1998 Red Hamer West Chester, Pa. United States of America

OF CHESTER COUNTY IV
Marc Reed Hamer
Illustrator

MISTY IS THE SCENE, not the mythical horse, in this strikingly beautiful sunrise graze near Lewisville in extreme southeastern Chester County. Just over the nearby Pennsylvania-Maryland border are the Fair Hill, Md. steeplechase grounds.

First Printing- 5,000 Copies- November, 1998

NICK SANTOLERI'S
Reaching for the Sky
painting appears on
Franklin's Metro Street
Atlas of Philadelphia
More of Santoleri on
page 62. Below, Karl
Kuerner's Full Service.

Table of Contents

Wyeth Put Us On The Map—Bollinger

Many years of off-again,on-again plotting went into the concept of this book embracing a cross-section of the artists of Chester County.

Not until we had focused sharply into the project had we discovered so many talented wielders of the brush-and so many of those setting up shop in the shadow of/master painter, Andrew Wyeth.

Rea Redifer, Karl Kuerner, Paul Scarborough, David Price, condo mates Patrick Kitson and Neil Carlin, Nancy Cunningham, George A. (Frolic) Weymouth and Christopher Schultz—all of whom appear in this volume—paint and live in proximity of the Route One corridor in Chadds Ford.

"We call this (Chadds Ford) the Garden of Eden with storm troopers (speeding cars) ," said Redifer—a description he shares with Wyeth.

Painters come to "the Garden" because it is one of America's beauty marks and because of the aura and consistently high level of work—over several decades—created by America's first family of art.

Wyeth inspired the local genre in many ways. Perhaps more than he knew.

"He put the rest of us on the map," declared landscape water colorist Richard Bollinger. "He put water color on a level it had never been before."

Wyeth spent so much time painting at the Kuerner farm in Chadds Ford his presence inspired the grandson of one of his most famous subjects to take to the brush.

The grandson, Karl J. Kuerner, evolved into an imaginative painter: who would dare to glorify the Chadds Ford Sunoco gas station at Christmas (opposite page)?

• • •

Kuerner said that Wyeth loved anonymity. One day he ran into an electrician, Henry Balestriere, in the Kuerner barn on Ring Road.

"Henry enters the barn and finds Andy painting away, "Kuerner related. "To Henry he was a just a nice older man. And while Henry was putting in the wiring, they had a light conversation. Henry thought to himself, "What a nice hobby to have when you're retired. And he's really not that bad!"

Eventually a lady friend of Andy's named Helga showed up. Henry then told Andy he had to go to get some supplies. "Good luck with your painting," he said.

Henry went up to the kitchen of the main house and spoke to Kuerner's father. "Who are all those people in the barn?" he asked. "They looked like they owned the place."

"Oh, you met Andy- Andy Wyeth," Mr. Kuerner replied.

"Oh my God! I had no idea," Henry blurted. "That was Andy Wyeth?"

" He flit all over the place in that jeep of his," said Kuerner. "Not bad for an 81 year old."

"He'll call ahead and then motor over just to chew the fat," said Bill Ewing, a nationally acclaimed portrait painter from Marshallton. "He's one of a kind. I've never seen a man throw paint against a canvas and come up with what he comes up with."

"He is excited when he paints somebody. He likes to come over and show us," said close friend George Sipala, whose third floor at his Painters Folly on Route One houses one of the Wyeth studios.

George helps stuff Andy into his Jeep and away he goes.

"He is the most frequently seen recluse in the country," dead panned Redifer.

• • •

Redifer, 63, spied Wyeth's work in New Orleans 40 years ago, wrote the artist a letter and came to Pennsylvania to meet him.

Rea walked down the lane to Andy's house, knocked on the door and so began an enduring friendship that would set all of Redifer's rich talents into bloom.

"He was a great influence," declared Redifer. "He was not a formal instructor per se, but a great task master. He said if I stayed in the area he would criticize my work. (That was in 1957)...I worked with Carolyn (Andy's late sister whose ability to teach art is legendary) in N.C.'s studio (see page 84). Quite a few times we went out in the field together. I learned more from him than anyone, but I appreciate him more as a friend than anything else."

George A. (Frolic) Weymouth, chairman of the board of trustees of Brandywine Conservancy in Chadds Ford, added:

"Andy spent a year putting together an exhibition of my work at the museum in 1995, unknown to me," said Frolic. "I was upset when I heard about it. But I was reminded that Andy had done so much for so many other artists, helping their careers...He's a wonderful, wonderful man."

One of the peaks of Scarbororgh's career occurred the night Andy and his wife Betsy purchased his portrait of pumpkins at the Chadds Ford Gallery.

"Most of the good artists," declared Jamison, "appreciate other artists' work. In teaching, you will learn from the 29 other artists around you."

• • •

Wyeth touched Jamison's life almost 40 years ago.

"Barclay Rubincam (the late West Chester realist) asked if he could take a couple of my pieces to a show at the Hotel duPont in Wilmington," Phil related. "I would ask maybe $25 apiece while Andy Wyeth had some on sale for between $450 and $700, which was a lot of money then.

"One of the volunteers said: 'How would anyone charge that kind of money for that. There's hardly any paint on the paper!'"

To which the show director replied: I know Andy Wyeth and I know his reputation and I can assure you that he is not selling paint by the gallon!"

Wyeth donated the proceeds from those paintings to the building of the Chester County Art Association building in West Chester.

SCOTT BOLLINGER, 19, summed up his three great loves at the Delaware County Christian School with this painting. Scott is the son of West Chester artist Ric Bollinger.

SPRING • SUMMER

6

..OFF TO THE WILLOWDALE RACES

UNBRIDLED HORSES race the carriages down the open country roads at the sound of the horn. Annual spring event starts at the Governeur Cadwalader's near Route 162 in Unionville and heads for the Willowdale steeplechase races where the coaches parade before, thousands.

THERE'S SOMETHING for everyone at the Willowdale Races at routes 926 and 82 between Kennett Square and Unionville—tail gate banquets, even for goats; picking wild flowers with a friend, showing off your immaculate Jack Russell terrier (right) or just watching the beautiful horses race on the flat and over the timber and brush.

CROWD OF OVER 6,000 watches the 1997 running of the Willowdale Races in perfect spring weather. The weather had much to do with preserving m'lady's fedora on the carriage ride home.

OT AIR BALLOONS light up the sky over the new shops at Ludwigs Corner,
ving contrast to a magnificent sunset.

At Home With The Coaching

JOHN AND RENIE LANDAN seemingly keep everything at home at their beautiful field stone estate on Chester Springs Road- their horses, their barns, their training ring (above right) and their advertising business (housed in a charming converted barn, partners in marriage, business and coaching, the Landans have been at the forefront of the fore-in-hand scene for years. Above, John drives an unusual random (three horses in a row) across the circular driveway of their lovely colonial home. Framed prints of many of Chester County's leading artists adorn their walls. The fireplace (right) is the focal point of the den.

Landans

THE DEVON HORSE SHOW (left) has been the scene of three of the Landans' marathon championships. Above, Mrs. Landan (blue suit) has her entire clan from children to grand children turned out and ready to board the coach for the 1998 competition. Below John Landan drives his unicorn (one horse in front of two) at the Ludwigs Corner Horse Show on Labor Day, 1997.

RAY CARR'S

RAYMOND H. CARR (center) took Chester County's antique car culture across the country and across the world in record-setting drives in 1994, 1996 and 1997. The Carrs' Saint Bernard (upper right) guards the 1902 Northern that Ray drove 2400 miles from San Diego, CA., to Jekyll Island, Ga., setting a Guiness record for driving the oldest car across America. He drove his 1909 Stanley Steamer (center) 5,041 miles from Anchorage, Alaska to Bar Harbor, Maine, in 1996 to celebrate the 100th anniversary of its invention by the Stanley twins. He participated in the longest rally in history for vintage cars in 1997 with the Peking to Paris adventure aboard his 1939 Ford Deluxe (above left). It covered 10,000 miles and 11 countries. He airs out his Steamer (left and right) on the long driveway of their Chester Springs home.

MAGNIFICENT MACHINES

Oldest Car to Cross America

NANCY CARR'S MAGNIFICENT INTERIOR

NANCY CARR went about decorating the Horseshoe Trail, Chester Springs home she shares with husband, Ray, and their Saint Bernard dog, Baron Von Heidrick, with the same exquisite taste she used on the Stotsville, Duling-Kurtz and Kennedy-Supplee Inns. In 1998 she finished decorating 220 bedrooms in their Lionville, Pa.-Holiday Inn. They also own the Bridgeport, N.J. Holiday Inn which has been nominated as one of the top 20 Holiday Inns in the world. Nancy has collected two prints by Chester

DECORATIONS

County artists each of the last 20 years at the Yellow Springs Art Show. They are exhibited throughout the home. Sandra Severson's portrait of their St. Bernard hangs over the fire place (lower left). Next to that photo is Nancy's life size doll house in which you can actually sit down for lunch. Dining is done more formally just off the kitchen and overlooking the pool (lower right) and around the pool and the pool house (right). Formal living room is at left.

THE ARTISTS

SUNRISE ON MARSH CREEK LAKE in the center of Chester County makes an incredibly beautiful subject for West Chester water color artist Richard Bollinger.

JUDY ANTONELLI

Judy Antonelli was 5 when she knew she wanted to be an artist.

The attractive West Chester brunette recalls sitting on a bench looking out the window at a glimmering poplar tree "and trying to get all of the colors with my 108 crayons."

The watercolorist's work is marked by its diversity of geography. "Retreats to paint have been the most wonderful highlights of my life," she said "Twice to Ireland, once to France, once to Cornwall in Devon, England. My father was a travel agent. He traveled everywhere. That's where I got my love of travel."

She wrote and colo illustrated "A Tribute t Victorian Cape May" i 1983, selling out 6,00 copies.

"I moved from Dela ware County to Cheste County just to paint it uniquely beautiful scen ery," she said. "I wante to live on Goshen Road The realtor said, 'Yo can't afford it, honey.' S we found a little niche o Williams Way" (just of Rt. 352) where her hus band, Bob, has establishe Antonelli's Framery an where she paints away, in spired by Monet an Renoir.

"Coming back fron Europe makes me appre

...ciate home so much. I have ...painted the beejabbers out ...of the place. Goshen Road ...s just beautiful. It is no ...wonder we have so many ...painters here.

Judy has been on the ...board of the Philadelphia ...Watercolor Club for 22 ...years. She teaches at the ...Wallingford Community ...Art Center, work shops at ...the Atlantic Community ...College, Cape May, NJ, ...Wayne, Pa. Art Center ...and the Chester County ...Art Association Center, ...West Chester, Pa.

She has been painting ...only originals since 1992.

VARIATIONS in Judy's focus: Chester County landscapes across the top, French street scene (middle left); wildlife (lower left), flowers in vase (left), and impressionistic oil (right). Photo (middle right) is of Goshen Road where she loves to paint.

RIC BOLLINGER looks over proofs of DAY'S END, the painting he created for Christmas, 1998. The water colorist's West Chester studio overlooks a wooded ravine which lends a peaceful atmosphere in which to create. INTERLUDE, right, was his fastest selling lithograph. Most of his landscapes feature snow and dramatic sunsets (above right).

RICHARD BOLLINGER

Richard Bollinger, 50, of West Chester, may have produced more watercolor work in Chester County in the last seven years than any other artist, according to one gallery owner.

Billing himself as "Painter of Rural America," Bollinger finds his inspiration in the Chester County Amish field stone, aesthetic snowfalls, dramatic sunsets and the rolling hills of his native county.

In recent years the silver haired father of four ventured to the nearby Chesapeake Bay and the old brick of Annapolis where his orginal paintings of city dock sold out in remarkable time.

Bollinger began his career as a commercial artist and graphic designer, for which he won many national awards. He began to develop his skills as a fine artist and in his first one-man show in 1976 at the Chadds Ford Gallery sold out all 26 original works.

"It was an Olympic year. With an advance from the gallery I went out and bought a TV so we could watch the Olympics."

In 1978 another one-man show at the same gallery (all landscapes) produced another sellout.

Of his more than 70 limited edition paintings, "Interlude," produced in 1994, was his fastest seller – 750 prints in five weeks. His originals, sold through galleries, bring between $10,000 and $12,000.

One of his more important commissions came from Valley Forge National Park. He depicted the Winter Encampment of 1777. His work has also been selected for the Winterthur, (DE.) Collection and the Embassy of the Arts Program conducted by the U.S. State Department.

The hallmark of his signatureare the letters TYL, abbreviation for "Thank you, Lord."

J. WAYNE BYSTROM

Early encouragement was the key for American realist painter J. Wayne Bystrom, 50, of Kennett Square. While attending Conestoga High School in Berwyn, Bystrom won the Main Line Women's Award for outstanding artist.

"It made me feel I had a shot," he said.

The former Marine went on to the Pennsylvania Academy of Fine Arts "where everybody worked in oils," and won more awards there than anybody in the academy's history.

But making a living at his "passion"

did not come easily. "I made $1700 my first year," he recalled, and had $900. in expenses. I worked harder than any time in my life.

Wayne and Pat Bystrom have been married 26 years but put off having children until 10 years ago "because I needed to establish myself as an artist to see if I would make it," Wayne said. "I didn't want any bitterness in my heart if I didn't make it."

Of Chester County artists, he says: "I think the world of these guys and their abili-

ties. But how do I survive in this area tha has so much talent? How do I fit in? It's scary It might all end tomorrow.

So Wayne went national and sells i two wholesale shows–Atlanta, Ga., and Ne York City.

"I take along 8 or 10 originals," h said. "Most will be Chester County scenes. And those scenes sell all over the nation.

He mails prints to more than 900 ga leries.

INFLUENCE of Thomas Kinkade, the Painter of Light, is seen in Bystrom's oil of John Chad House, above is so much a part of Bystrom's art (left panel).

"MY HOBBY is my family," say Bystrom--wife Pat of 24 years, son Christopher, 8, and daughter Brittany, 10, gathered with artist in his Kennett Square studio.

NO RAPIDS in artist's version of Pine Creek in Chester Springs.

NEILSON M. CARLIN

Visions of a life as an artist come early to many, so it was with portrait oil painter Neil Carlin, 27, who grew up outside West Chester. He began by drawing comic books in high school. In 1997 he launched the Renaissance Portrait Studio through which he has been working on private commissions.

"The attainment of a likeness, the elusive goal that has been a bane of many artists, is but the beginning of a portrait and not its conclusion," he has written.

"The artist must pass beyond the threshold of mimetic reproduction and reflect the dignity and nobility that lies within the heart."

Many of his portraits are of historical figures such as General William Tecumseh Sherman and Abraham Lincoln, the latter on view in the executive lobby of the new Genesis Health System building, Kennett Square, Pa.

Neil developed his penchant for painting historic figures at the University of the Arts, Philadelphia, where he earned a bachelor of fine arts degree in 1992.

Now, as a cultivated disciple of classical realism, this brilliant young talent is sought after by corporations, design firms and book publishers for his work. His most recent endeavor includes opening The Brandywine Atelier, a school of private art instruction located in Kennett Square.

NEIL CARLIN (right) with friend and fellow artist Patrick Kitson outside condo they share in Kennett Square. They also share Alaskan husky, Timber.

CARLIN covers up in his basement studio.

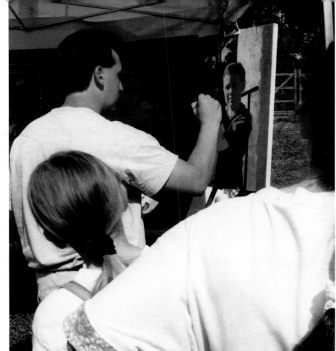

INTEREST IN CIVIL WAR resulted in Drummer Boy, left. Portrait above is of grandfather, Larry DeSimone of Cochranville. Working at Chadds Ford Days, 1998, (top of page) draws a crowd.

NANCY CUNNINGHAM

Nancy Cunningham, of Chadds Ford, was a tiny little girl when she first sketched her classmates on the school bus. And when the nuns wanted some decorative art on the walls, they always sought out Nancy, who became known in school as "the artist."

It was a gift from God, she said, a talent that would surface in the genes of her son, Richard.

"He was drawing rocket ships when he could barely hold a pencil," she recalled. Today, Richard has blossomed into an artist-architect and owns Cunningham Design, Inc.

Meanwhile, mom's lovely landscapes can be seen in numerous galleries and private collections throughout the U.S. and abroad and in corporate places such as the Wilmington Trust Co., Bank of Delaware, Maryland Bank and the Chadds Ford Winery.

Energized by picturesque surroundings, this graduate of the Moore College of Art, Philadelphia, has painted seriously for 17 years. Her first exhibit as an adult was at the Chadds Ford elementary school which her children attended.

John McCoy, married to Anne Wyeth, did the judging that year and Nancy won "a second or a third place." That was an oil but she would soon switch to watercolor as a medium.

In 1991 she would have a one-woman show at the Chadds Ford Gallery where she would present 30 original paintings.

Nancy's favorite painting season is spring. She has a propensity for highlighting historic buildings with shades of pink flowers, most notably hot pink.

In painting historic sites such as the Brinton 1704 House (bottom right) or landscapes at Longwood Gardens, it is her way of "paying homage to the area she has come to love and respect."

LOVE TEMPLE remarque replicates the real structure at Longwood Gardens (left).

COUNTRY GARDEN was Nancy's first limited edition reproduction.

NANCY sketches Peirce House (far left) at Longwood Gardens. Peirce family in 1798 founded one of America's first arboretums. Canada geese are year 'round residents at the love temple.

MAX is Jean E. Diver's biggest fan, checking out the artistic nuances in Jean's Romeo and Juliet scene (above). Below, a dress up tea for two very young ladies. Jean dresses up in her favorite fedora (right).

JEAN E. DIVER

When you enter Jean Diver's Landenberg, PA.,
dio-home you are struck by the diversity of her
…much of it in the process of being completed.

Near the ceiling is a wild abstract; over there hangs
cene out of Romeo and Juliet; in another room ballet
ncers; a horse eating out of a bucket, its mane and
brushed by backlighting; an unfinished pencil draw-
of a Middle Eastern woman ("she will eventually
ve a veil").

Running around on the hardwood floor is tabby
, Toulouse, short for Toulouse Lautrec; and a Jack
ssell terrier, Max, short for master artist Maxwell
rrish.

"To be a master, you need to do whacky, off-the
ll painting," says Diver, 36. But in the next moment
adds: "I think realism is coming back."

Mythology, symbolism, unique soulful expression;
ferent from everyone else. These are terms she uses
describe HER art.

N.C. Wyeth has been an on-going inspiration; so
J.W. Waterhouse, a romantic classicist from En-
nd; and Parrish. Also Degas, famous for his horse
d ballet paintings.

"I love the movement of the ballet, the horses," she
d. "I have studied the masters. But because you have
died under a painter, it doesn't mean that they have
ght you anything. They are there to offer you tech-
al advice…But I definitely aspire to be soulful in my
rk, rather than paint just a pretty picture."

Funny she would say that. Her paintings are drop
d beautiful. But soulful.

And after 14 years of formal study, 10 years of solo
d group exhibitions from Palm Beach, FL. to New
rk City- and the acquisition of an agent there in 1998-
r future looks bright.

DUNN, early in career.

HARRY DUNN checks the visitor list at the Sunset Hill Gallery in downtown West Chester. Dunn's painting of his favorite gallery is at right. Photo below shows his best friend Tom Andress and gallery owner Sandy Riper greeting each other.

34

NUNS AT PLAY, doing flips.

THE HEN PARTY

HARRY DUNN 1929 • 1998

As an art colony, Chester County could called the University of Diversity. And inters like Harry Dunn, 69, who passed ay on June 9, 1998 in his home town of st Chester, helped make it so.

Throughout his entire life, Harry was licted with an acute sense of humor. And oured out spontaneously onto his draw- board.

Among his repertoire of subjects were dmarks such as borough buildings and nts such as fox hunts, but he majored in painting nuns and old ladies en farce.

"In the 60's women were absolutely insulted the way he depicted them," declared Tom Andress, Harry's lifelong friend. "Now they laugh at themselves. With the nuns, he wanted to show they were human, too.

"But Harry was extremely unpredictable and impulsive. When he turned on the Gershwin – he loved show tunes – and sat down to point, you never knew what was circulating in that brain."

Dunn worked in the unpretentious basement of a home he and Tom shared on Sharpless Street in West Chester, right up until 1997 when a nerve and muscle disorder halted his one of a kind talent.

But Harry, who scheduled himself into at least six hours of work a day, left behind a mountain of work which ensured the continuation of Christmas shows at his favorite gallery, Sunset Hill, in downtown West Chester. He had 15 spring and winter shows there, but was also represented by major galleries in New York and Philadelphia, helped develop the NBC peacock, designed greeting cards for Hallmark and painted his way into McCalls and True magazines.

One of his early teachers was Carolyn Wyeth, of Chadds Ford, with whom he studied at the Philadelphia College of Art after graduating from West Chester High School in 1949.

MATRONS AT PLAY (above), a self-portrait (right) and downtown West Chester.

MY CHILDHOOD DAYS

WILLLIAM

How do you go from a drag racer i
high school to one of the nation's leadir
portrait and still life painters?

How do you go from a drag racer i
high school to one of the nation's leadir
portrait and still life painters?

William O. Ewing III, of Marshalto
Pa., has experienced that 180 degree turr
"The Unionville boys hated me for drivir
all the girls home in ninth grade," recalle
Bill, now 50. "In fact, drag racing got m
kicked out of school. I transferred
Kennett High and graduated from there.

Then came the BIG DECISION. "M
girl friend was going off to college. I wa
going nowhere (except maybe to becomir
a grease monkey).

"My dad sat me down. He said if v
got married I would wake up to someboc
who had a college degree. I would ha
nothing. He set the whole scene for me
20 minutes."

From that pivotal talk, Bill went on a
education binge, earning a Bachelor
Fine Arts from Tennessee, a master of Fir
Arts from Idaho, two years at the Pa. Aca

BILL AND MARY EWING'S HOME is very masculine. It rambles all over a hill near Marshalton. You can see Unionville six miles away in the winter. The wood work is exquisite. The open ended fireplace is immense. Bill has carved a classic Chevy convertible in half to create a bar. Their bedroom is a loft over Bill's head on the balcony.

O. EWING III

ny of Fine Arts under Albert de Costa and year's tour of Europe where he focused on the work of the great Flemish paint-rs. He found his way back to Chester ounty, did some commercial work for ad-rtising agencies and began painting iends and acquaintances of friends.

"One day I was painting the chairman the board of Conrail and I met Mary, his cretary. I bugged her for six months be-re she went out with me. Now I'm a newly ed. I didn't realize I had so much respect r some one. That's the key, I guess."

Ewing estimates he has done about 300 portraits over the years. Old masters embrandt and Rubens inspired him. And e Frenchman Eugene de la Croix. "They ere great technicians," he said.

Bill has won many awards. His work ay be appreciated at the David David allery, Philadelphia and the Somerville anning Gallery, Greenville, Delaware.

THE ARTIST studies an unfinished portrait.

EWING's late father, William II, and mother, Helen.

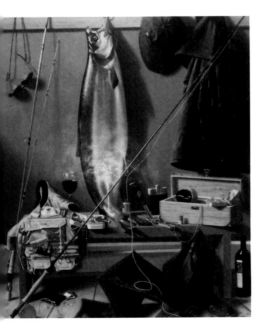

A STILL LIFE called Smoked Salmon. See if you can find the smoking cigar.

EWING, who owns "13 or 14" antique cars puffs away in his basement repair shop.

CHARLES JAY

"**I** don't do still life. I don't do portraits or land-scapes. I basically just paint flowers."

Thus, at age 50, did Charles Jay describe a choice of subject that has fascinated him ever since he was a kid. And a subject he became noted for in the 22 years he lived at 126 E. Barnard St., West Chester until 1994.

He has since returned to Morton, Pa. "to take care of my mother."

However, the gifted oil painter continues to have showings at Sunset Gallery, West Chester. His average painting is 36 by 24 and is priced between $3,000 and $5,000. He sells only originals.

"I started drawing as a kid," noted Jay. "I just always like to draw. Nobody ever had to encourage me."

He had some formal training at the Pennsylvania School of Fine Arts for one year. There was a class for clay, which he rejected and a class for drawing under Arthur De Costa. "We at first tried statues," said Jay. "No good."

"When I paint flowers," he said, "I just make things up. I keep adding a flower until the vase is filled up."

West Chester's Philip Jamison, whose flower por-traits are legendary, would oversee some of Jay's work from time to time.

"He would wear this big black coat to his open-ings," noted Jamison. "On the coat were big white de-signs. He would top it off with a derby hat. Charles is quiet, but a character."

The highlight of Jay's career came in 1981-83 when a Chester County family invited him to their home in Paris after one of his paintings won a prize at their Duncan Gallery in New York.

"I did some painting over there and I got to see the

VIBRANT is one way to describe Charles Jay's flower portraits in oil as he stands outside his old studio at 126 E. Barnard St., West Chester. He had a room on the third floor.

CHARLES JAY chats with former E. Barnard St. West Chester neighbor.

Old Masters' work at the Louvre. It made an impression on me. I like them but I don't paint like those guys. Mr. De Costa would tell you that."

MARTHA FENOGLIO

Martha Fenoglio, Birmingham Township, came to Chester County via Maryland, Connecticut and then Wilmington, De.

We discovered her painting of Rt.82 at Sestrtich's Market in Unionville in 1998.

Like many of the artists, she paints her surroundings—200 watercolors over the years—including a lot of commission work. Martha got her start as a fifth grader at Ellicott City, MD. when she produced a pen and ink of a vase. A local portrait painter advised her mother to give her lessons. And she has been painting landscapes, stuffed animals, flowers and portraits (as seen below) ever since.

Both of her and Dick Fenoglios's children, Mark and Judy, graduated from Unionville High. Both had a talent for art.

Mark, like his dad, works for duPont. Judy, a talented volleyball player, was tragically killed when her car hydroplaned in a rainstorm coming home from a tournament. It happened within two weeks of completion of the fall painting of Unionville.

Martha finally completed it 10 months later.

AS VIEWED through a wide angle lens, Martha Fenoglio's Route 82 as it runs through Unionville in the spring (above) and in the autumn (below).

SANDRA GIANGIULIO

SANDRA GIANGIULIO stands in front of her floral painting, "Monet's Bouquet,' which she sold at a show in Valley Forge when this photo was taken in 1998. The inspiration for the water color came from her visit to Monet's Garden about an hour outside Paris. Painters from all over the world visit the beautiful gardens of the late master artist. Sandra was visiting with her son in Paris who was attending Cordon B'leu, the world famous cooking school.

RAPP'S DAM BRIDGE, Kimberton.

Sandra Giangiulio has had three lives.

One, as an actress and singer in summer stock and night clubs, first performing with Ginger Rogers.

Two, bearing three children.

Three, painting, after the children started school.

Sandra studied under world renown John Pike, whose art appeared on TRUE magazine, and nationally known Dominic Di Stefano, of Upper Darby.

The Kimberton resident paints "here, there and everywhere," including New England and Europe.

The American Cancer Society selected her "Valley Forge Farm" (right) as one of four greeting cards for 1989.

Her Kimberton Post Office (lower right) was painted in commemoration of that structure's 200th anniversary in 1996.

Her Boat House Row prints are very popular as is Sandra's rendition: "Great Days at Cape May," a montage of nine houses in that New Jersey resort town which sells well today even though she created it in 1989 for the Philadelphia Art Show.

"I used to do 100 paintings a year," declared Sandra.

At press time she was working on a five-foot wide painting at Ridley Creek State Partk as a fund raiser for the cancer unit of the Chester-Crozer Medical Center.

Sandra is a seven year survivor of cancer, from which she is free.

VALLEY FORGE FARM overlooking Knox Covered Bridge.

KIMBERTON POST OFFICE, 200 years old in 1996.

41

HOUSE OF ART- The walls and floors (lower left) of the Jamison's cozy West Chester home are laden with art, theirs and everybody else's. Phil's watercolor of a Downingtown RR crossing graces an easel. His <u>Capturing Nature in Watercolor</u> is opened to a landscape of downtown West Chester.

PHILIP AND JANE JAMISON

PHIL AND JANE JAMISON in their upstairs studio and gallery.

Philip and Jane Jamison's home at 104 ~ice Street, West Chester, may say more ~out the artful couple than any words.

Their home is adorned with Bertoia ~ulpture, many paintings by other artists, ~tiques, art books galore and pots of his ~nature daisies — the paintings of which ~ has become renown.

The couple moved into their c 1875 ~me 20 years ago from a stone farm house ~st outside of town.

Jane and Phil met in first grade. "She ~ught me how to paint," smiled Phil. "He ~s cute even then," said Jane.

They raised twin daughters and a son, ~ artistically inclined.

"I don't have too many of my own paint-~gs hanging around," said Phil, who ~thored two books on painting, " b e -~se that reminds me of work. When it's

hanging in front of you, you always want to change it.

"I'd rather enjoy somebody else's work. And it's a good investment."

The first painting he collected was a Horace Pippin — the late black stylist — a painting of West Chester's Gen. Smedley Butler.

Phil's reputation as an artist has brought him offers to teach at watercolor societies all over the country "But I decided long ago (he's in his 70's) I was either going to teach or paint, and I decided on the latter."

William Palmer Lear was his art teacher in junior and senior high school in West Chester and was the "source of wisdom" that projected him to the Philadelphia Museum School of Art where he met W. Emerton Heitland, a water color instructor who directed him into an ultra successful

career.

Phil has exhibited at the Philadelphia Museum of Art, the Boston Museum of Art, the National Academy of Design – a prestigious body of which he is a member; and in the show, 200 Years of Watercolor Painting in America at the Metropolitan Museum of Art in New York.

He has had nine 1-man exhibitions at the Hirschl and Adler Galleries in New York City, is listed in Who's Who in America and Who's Who in American Art.

Wrote Bruce St. John, director of the Delaware Art Museum: "Philip Jamison . . . has the sensitivity to fill his work with a poetic quality that is closely related to beautiful music."

Jane Jamison seconds that thought.

JANE'S painting of their Maine escape (left) and her window view of South Church St. from their home

JACK KAISER uses "a lot of contrasting washes on top of each other..people say it is a lot richer than most water colors." The initial washes can be seen in his studio (left). Rustic artifacts of a country porch (right) become fodder for Kaiser's brush.

FOUNDRY AND NAILERS' ROW, beginning of Phoenix Iron and Steel Co., Phoenixville.

SEACRIST NEWS AGENCY, and downtown lunch spot, Phoenixville.

44

JACK R. KAISER

BIRCH RUN ROAD makes a perfect path for a bike ride for artist Jack Kaiser, right on past his 200-year old Birchrunville house (left).

Andrew Wyeth inspired the first 15 years of Jack R. Kaiser's painting. "But once I started to read art history," declared the Birchrunville resident, "I started to diverge."

His colors have a richness that have become a trademark for the self taught artist.

"Variety of subjects, warmth of light, warmth of feel, something delicate . . . that's why he has a tremendous following," declared Liz Trumper, who manages the Virginia Lippincott Gallery in Phoenixville where Kaiser's work has been on display since 1987.

Mrs. Lippincott, Trumper's mother, co-chaired and founded the prestigious Yellow Springs Art Show.

Top price for any of Kaiser's originals is $1,200, extremely low in the 1998 market. Another reason for his popularity is that he focuses his eye on a specific region such as Phoenixville, where he endears himself to the populace by painting familiar buildings and points of interest.

"My father was a lithographer so we were all interested in art," he said of his family. "I used to paint from 9 at night until 2 in the morning. Now, as a fulltime painter, I have all day. And if I get going on a couple of pieces I can go for 3 days without any sleep."

Kaiser, 55, paints 40 to 50 pictures a year, mostly landscapes.

As this book went to press, he prepared for a 1-man show at the Chester County Art Association, West Chester.

FRENCH CREEK above Sheeders Mill shows radiance of color as he retreated from Wyeth's early influence. **ANGELUS BELL** (right) went into the permanent collection of the Berman Gallery at Ursinus College, Collegeville.

RICH RED HIGHLIGHTS find their way into all three of Millie's paintings on this page, and into the American flag along St. Peters Village (right).

MILDRED SANDS KRATZ

It all began in 1956 when the adopted twins arrived.

"It was a gift and a blessing," declared Mildred Sands Kratz some 42 years and 2,500 paintings later. The necessity of staying home with her babies meant she had to study and paint.

It was the start of a long and honored career that carried this athletic lady (her sport is tennis) through 130 one-woman shows from 1963 to 1992.

The highlight for this watercolorist supreme came in the early 1970's when she landed a one-person show at Gallery Madison 90 in New York City. Four more shows ensued and she is represented by that gallery today.

"If you can make it in New York, you can make it anywhere," and she certainly did.

"This is all I did," Millie said. "I gave up everything to paint."

She once had a studio on the second floor above the general store in St. Peters Village (she painted in the village below). She sold her first painting to the postmaster for $12. In 1998 – 40 years later – she received $10,000 for an original.

Another early memory: in 1960 she entered a Motorola contest in West Chester at Murray's, Gay and Church St. Jamie Wyeth, 13, won first prize. But Millie came back a year later and not only captured the blue ribbon locally but won the National Motorola prize.

Seven months of the year she resides in New Tampa, Fl. with her husband, Red Johnson, who is an accomplished decoy and song-bird carver.

WATER COLOR ARTIST is Millie's vanity license plate (above). Below, her beloved St. Peters Village near Rt. 23 in northwestern Chester County, the site of most of her paintings.

EYES OF THE FOREST- timber wolf in upstate New York.

SUNSHOWER- find the great blue heron (above).

THE TERRITORY AHEAD- timber wolves again in upstate New York (below).

PATRICK E. KITSON

ARTIST IN HIS STUDIO- Kitson works on painting for Stone Harbor, N.J. wildlife show.

Patrick Kitson, 28, will likely become, one of America's premiere landscape and wildlife painters. His medium is oil.

"He is so good it is scary," said Richard Bollinger, one of Chester County's most prolific artists.

Kitson grew up in central New Jersey, graduated from The University of the Arts, Philadelphia, and moved into a condo with his schoolmate and fellow artist Neil Carlin in Kennett Square, Pa.

"I just fell in love with the area," said Kitson, who has the room at the top for his studio while Carlin paints his models in the basement.

"I just followed the art movement here which was sort of lacking in New Jersey." Kitson was inspired however, in his pre-teen years by internationally known sculptor Donald DeLue, painter F. Travers Neidlinger, and nationally known illustrator Peter Carras – all of whom either lived next door or in back of him.

It was here that Kitson learned the importance of an artistic community and its nurturing influences.

"I got my hands in clay at DeLue's and took a lot of painting lessons from Neidlinger,' he said. In the meantime his grandparents took him on cross country trips – one to Yellowstone National Park which "cultivated a love for nature and wildlife."

At 23, he was invited to exhibit his work at Prestige Gallery in Canada alongside several world-renowned wildlife artists including Robert Batemen, Carl Brenders and John Seerey-Lester.

He has done collector plate work for the Franklin Mint, Media, Pa. when they needed an artist to produce "very fine detail."

But his main thrust is the galleries. His repertoire of originals sell for as much as $13,000.

EVENING HUNT- red tailed hawk (above).
NORTHEASTERN REFLECTIONS- Canada geese (left)
INDIAN SUMMER (above left)

Andrew Wyeth's influence as an artist had no greater effect in the Chadds Ford area than on Karl J. Kuerner.

Karl, 41, is the grandson of two of the master's storied subjects, Anna and Karl Kuerner. Karl and his wife Louise live on top of a hill across from the grandparents' farm. It was as a child that Karl became fascinated with Wyeth's preoccupation with the Kuerner homestead as subjects for his paintings.

So, Karl, in his pre-teen years, tried his hand at painting and his dad took the work to show Carolyn Wyeth, Andrew's sister and legendary teacher in the area.

"The first thing that Carolyn said," recalled Karl, "was to go home and paint something that you love. That's exactly what Andy would say. Carolyn just gently pushed me along . . . this is nice, do this to make it stronger. Of course, she couldn't give me the passion. That comes from within."

Young Karl studied under Carolyn from age 13 to 20. And also at the Art Institute of Philadelphia. He began teaching at the Darlington Fine Arts Center, Wawa, Pa., in 1980.

"I teach at night, paint in the morning and farm (his 50 acres) in the afternoon (raising, cutting and baling hay)."

Twenty-five of his paintings are of his wife, Louise. They had their wedding reception at Big Bend, at the invitation of owner Frolic Weymouth. "He is very sharing with everyone in his own way," said Louise of the artist and director of the Brandywine Conservancy.

In training her percheron, Dentzel (named after a German carousel horse carver), Louise would drive her cart to Frolic's, three miles away, and then another nine miles to Winterthur where they would parade at the steeplechase races the first Sunday in May.

Passing by Frolic's gave Karl the inspiration to paint Just Passing By (above).

KARL J. KUERNER

JUST PASSING BY, the title of the work to which Karl J. Kuerner is applying the finishing touches (left) is re-enacted by his wife Louise and white percheron Dentzel at Frolic Weymouth's Big Bend estate, Chadds Ford, above and below.

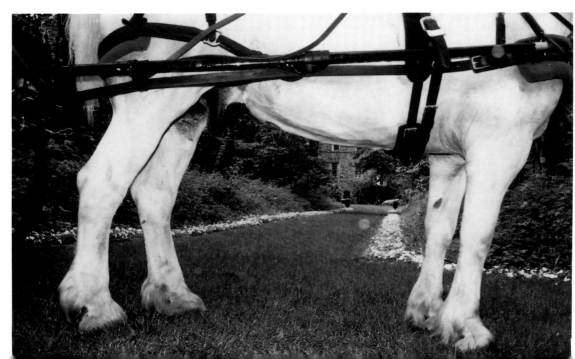

51

VIEW FROM A STUDIO- When Karl Kuerner paints, he looks to his right at this view of the Kuerner barn on Ring Road (left). The barn is mostly full of hay bales, stacked fireplace wood, antique carts (below) and lots of cobwebs (right). Two paintings are of his wife, Louise, one in a Halloween hat, the other with baby muskrats that invaded their home (far right), and one with the family cat ready to pounce.

TWO MORE views of Kuerner barn, one from the top of the hill where Karl and Louise reside. Old Kuerner homestead, painted by Andrew Wyeth inside and out (above). Below, white percheron Dentzel looks across Ring Road with Lousie and author aboard the cart. Hill leading to artist's home lies ahead. Nearby, N. C. Wyeth and grandson Newell, 3, were killed when their car stalled on this road at a railroad crossing and a train crushed it. It happened Oct. 19, 1945.

MARTIN MAY

PEN AND INK artist Martin May, of Romansville, chats with customer during "Super Sunday" in downtown West Chester. May's portrait of old Warner Theatre (below) contrasts with 1998 look as suburban home of Phila. Inquirer, antique car exhibition in foreground.

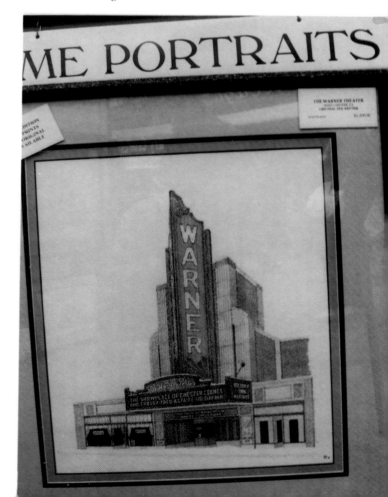

DIAMOND ROCK SCHOOL in Valley Forge (above). Linda McNeil at home with Alex (right).

SETTLED IN- typical winter scene in Chester County, except this is Vermont.

FLORAL FANTASY, inspired by her West Chester garden, left photo and right. Those are her husband's boots.

LINDA McNEIL

SUMMER REPOSE reflects the kaleidoscope of colors that consistency flow into contrasting bouquets from Linda McNeil's palette.

Each summer Linda McNeil, of Lionville, takes off around the countryside and uncovers scenes which she will want to photograph in the winter.

"As I meander down the road," she said, "I am constantly enthralled with the variety of wildflowers that line the highways.

"One summer I was enjoying the backroads of Chester County and was constantly overcome with the abundance of daisies, Queen Anne's lace, chicory, clovers, crown vetch . . . just so many weeds to most people.

"I stopped my car and sketched a variety of these flowers. Later that day I created FLORAL FANTASY (below)."

Linda has had more than 300 watercolors accepted in national and international juried shows. In addition to flowers she likes to paint wildlife and historical sites. Some of these are Lafayette headquarters in Chadds Ford, Knox Covered Bridge and the octagonal Diamond Rock School in Valley Forge, Jenny Lind spring house, Rapps Dam Covered Bridge, Great Valley Mill and Birmingham octagonal school.

Her own garden, complete with a fish pond, has inspired many of her paintings. "It is an old fashioned garden as I remember it from my grandmother's yard," she said.

GATEWAY TO BIG BEND- David had been at this painting-the Brandywine approaching Frolic Weymouth's Big Bend- for two weeks. "It needs highlights in the sky, on the rapids and something in the front, maybe a plough horse," she said. His easel is home made.

SKETCHES line Price's studio wall (left). Palettes with his special mix of oils (above).

DAVID PRICE

David Price grew up on the Brandywine and he knew "somewhere along the line I was going to paint it . . . from memory . . . in the old world style."

He did. And in 1983 upon the occasion of a one-man show at the Chadds Ford Gallery, he sold all 15 of his oil paintings in a half hour.

You would think that success would spur Price onto a new surge of painting. It did not.

He and his wife, Lynn, had another business: Chadds Ford Cabinets. She designed them. He made them. And it provided a steady income from which to raise their two small children.

• • •

Now those children are in their 20's, and the silver haired artist is back at his true love, painting in the style of the Flemish masters.

"I've been using it (the Maroger medium) as long as I've been painting," declared Price, now 50. "In the 70's I went to York Academy of Arts. My mentor, Ted Fitzkee, taught me the technique. It was what I was after."

Price buys his Maroger tubes of oil in Pittsburgh (even the large art stores in Philadelphia don't have it, he said). The medium is named after Jacques Maroger, a French painter and restorer who wrote the book <u>The Secret Mediums and Techniques of the Masters</u>.

Price adds linseed oil, litharge (a type of lead oxide), and mastic tears, a granule that falls out of trees along the Mediterranean. The latter costs $55 an ounce and gives a Flemish gloss to his painting. Adding beeswax instead of mastic tears would give more of an Italian finish – less gloss.

He cooks these ingredients in a porcelain pot until he has a quart. "I made my last batch in April, 1997" she said.

The Maroger tubes of oil come in many colors, of course.

He adds the other ingredients 50-50 with the Maroger to attain the mix that he brushes on to his stretched canvas.

• • •

"The old masters didn't have it too easy," he said. "They didn't squeeze it (the oil paint) out of a tube."

Bill Ewing, a portrait painter from Marshalton, also uses the Maroger medium.

David and Lynn reside in Hamorton, 2 miles east of Longwood Gardens, flat dab on Route One. Their house was built in 1860 by a country buggy doctor, John Weadle.

David and Lynn are also best friends with Karl and Louise Kuerner, the artist family from Ring Road.

"We have completely different styles," said David. (Karl works mostly in acrylics). "But when I hit on something . . . I get my heart on that canvas, I call him and tell him to get over here. He does the same with me."

ANOTHER VIEW of Brandywine (above). Pet cat cries for attention in Price's hallway (right). Home along Rt. 1 in Hamorton was built in 1860.

STUDENT Bill Ewing's oil of Redifer (upper left). Clockwise, Redifer's Lincoln entitled <u>The Burden</u>; British soldier traversing the Brandywine painted by Redifer for the back cover of the 200th anniversary booklet commemorating the Battle of the Brandywine (front cover, right); war bride during World War I in Rea's award winning <u>ONCE UPON A CANVAS SKY</u> (far right).

REA REDIFER on his 64th birthday, June 10, 1998.

THE MANY FACES OF REA REDIFER

If Rea Redifer were a quarterback, he would be of the multiple threat variety. He would run the option, pass, punt, block, lateral, catch passes, and tackle – if necessary.

But Redifer, 64, is a multiple threat artist.. And, as such, he has no equal in this artists' colony.

The Kennett Square resident is a book author, film writer, speech writer, actor, historian, art teacher "extraordinaire" and painter in the Andrew Wyeth tradition.

"But there's a $6 million difference," retorted Redifer, whose work has often been compared to Wyeth's.

"I don't paint for the market," he said. "I paint for myself." Pretty much the way Wyeth does it.

"He has been a great influence," adds Redifer of his friend and counselor of over 40 years. "I am not a pretty picture painter (either). I am interested in the psychological."

Example: there are two sides to Redifer's Lincoln entitled The Burden, painted in 1994. "He's frightened on the right side," said Rea, "and serene on the left."

Redifer, a Civil War buff, said that when Lincoln was nine he was kicked in the head by a mule. "He had a wandering eye when he became tired," and it shows in many of his Lincoln paintings.

He wrote and illustrated a book Once Upon A Canvas Sky, which earned the National Space and Aviation Writers book award in 1984. It translated in brute realism the air war over Europe during World War I.

Said Wyeth of the illustrations: "These paintings are among the finest of their genre that I have seen. They go beyond mere illustration and live on their own."

Redifer wrote and produced three films with Denys McCoy: An American Memory (a train ride across America); The Last Escape of Billy the Kid, featuring Jack Elam and Steve Railsback; and The Last Rebel, in which Joe Namath performed just after winning the Super Bowl.

Rea wrote narrations for Jim McKay, celebrating in film the 100th anniversary of the Maryland Hunt Cup; for Burgess Meredith (the trainer in Rocky); and Claude Rains.

I was always torn between the painting, the novels and the film business," said Rea. "The film business is a 24 hour business. Writing a film play is like re-writing a novel 12 times. . . I was too much of a maverick to work that kind of thing out (concentrating on one form of art)."

Rea has a twin brother, Rex, who became " a great cartoonist and feature writer for the Indianapolis Star. The art bug got to us when we were little kids."

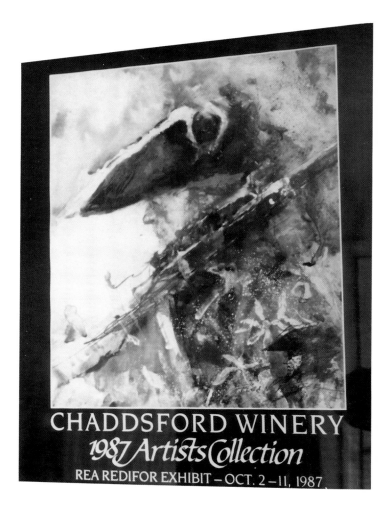

CHADDSFORD WINERY
1987 Artists Collection
REA REDIFOR EXHIBIT – OCT. 2 –11, 1987

THE BATTLE OF BRANDYWINE
1777-1977 CHADDS FORD, PENNSYLVANIA

ONCE UPON A CANVAS SKY

NICK SANTOLERI'S artful rendition of the Hicks Farm on Airport Road, West Goshen Township (far right) is duplicated by photographs on a spring day in 1998. Fence at right was photographed on Goshen Road near the Radnor Hunt and used as the guide for painting (far right).

NICHOLAS P. SANTOLERI

Just about everything Nick Santoleri paints has stone in it.

Possibly that's because the 41-year-old West Chester native was a fulltime stone mason. Ten years ago he became a fulltime painter.

"As my masonry business closed down for the winter," said the mustachioed Santoleri, "I went back into painting."

Today, his work which mostly consists of historical landmarks and open country reflecting the beauty of his early ties to Chester County, is represented in nearly 500 galleries and framing shops across the United States.

Nick can name just about every type of stone in Pennsylvania.

"The obelisk at Penn State (in Centre County) has stone from all over the state," he noted. "Chester County has serpentine stone and the Hicks property in West Goshen (reflected in the photos and paintings on these pages) is the best example of Chester County field stone.

"Painting (which he started to excel at in high school) used to be a hobby. The first painting took me two years. Now, if I have a deadline, it takes me 45 days." He gets between $6,000 and $8,000 for his originals.

Nick is well know for painting the cov-

ers of the eight street atlases of the Philadelphia area published by Franklin Maps.

Santoleri considers Peter Sculthorpe, who painted out of Unionville and now lives in Rockland, De., a "mentor."

"He contributed more than he thinks." Said Nick. "If it wasn't for him I would not be a fulltime artist. We (other Chester County artists) were all driving through the fog and his were the taillights we followed."

Sculthorpe, a few years older than Nick and also a product of the West Chester school district, is not only a supreme artist of American realism but an extremely hard working marketer of his work.

Contentment Found is title of painting at right. **A View of the Hunt** (below) features reynard and fox hunters (if you look closely).

QUIET MORNING, a recent artwork accompanied by a Scarborough verse: "If only I could paint the sounds of a quiet morning...then I would be able to capture something beyond the frame."

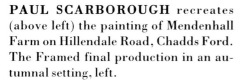

PAUL SCARBOROUGH recreates (above left) the painting of Mendenhall Farm on Hillendale Road, Chadds Ford. The Framed final production in an autumnal setting, left.

ROUTE 100 NORTH in Chadds Ford, featuring Christian Sanderson Museum, is one of Paul's more popular paintings.

When you go looking for Paul Scarborough's barn-studio on Brinton Bridge Road in Chadds Ford, you better remember the number of bumps in the road. He tells you there are three bumps coming off Rt. 1, but if you miss the third bump you're in the next township.

But it is a great place to get lost, and so reflective of this man's lovely pastoral watercolor and acrylic paintings.

Scarborough, 51, is a towering, solidly built 6-5 and seems even taller in his trademark cowboy hat. But his size belies his sensitive nature.

"When people look at a Paul Scarborough painting, I hope it tells them about me – the things I'm sensitive to; the flight of a bird, a sunny day; the kind of people I have as friends and places I find interesting," he said.

Certainly the lifelong bachelor has created immense respect for his work. Painting professionally since 1969, he has exhibited widely on the East coast in one man and group shows; and every two years at the Chadds Ford Gallery where he generally sells out of between 35 or 40 paintings.

At one such show, Andrew and Betsy Wyeth came early and stayed late. "It was just terrific that they came," said Scarborough. "And on top of that they bought a painting. The subject was pumpkins. Andy likes to carve pumpkins."

That was 1985. In the same year Paul was chosen to paint the flight of the space shuttle Atlantis.

WENDY SCHEIRER

Gardens and flowers are close to Wendy Scheirer's heart. So when the West Chester artist was asked for a representational site in which she worked, she selected Joanna Reed's Longview Farm, Bodine Road, Malvern.

All of the photographs on these pages are of the gardens of the nationally know horticulturalist.

The paintings of the barn and the side view of the farm house are by Wendy, matched by photos of same.

Ms. Reed and her late husband met at the Philadelphia Academy of Art, explained Wendy. They intended the property to be an art studio. "I came out here to paint, but never did," said Joanna, whose husband, George, died in 1982.

Her garden became her art work.

And even at 81 on a hot spring day when these photos were made, she was busy weeding and cultivating around this beautifully arranged panoply of color. Just the kind of intense color Ms. Scheirer loves to paint.

Hagley Museum has hung two of Wendy's paintings and put them into print – the estate and gardens of the original DuPont Mills.

SNOW SCENES and authentic history abound in the art work of Christopher Schultz. Exquisite examples are <u>APPLE SEED HOLLOW</u> (Mercer's Mills 1744) above, and <u>APPLE GROVE SLEIGH RIDE</u>, left. Thomas Downing, founder of Downingtown, and Caleb Pierce, an engineer, created the mills along the Octorara near Atglen. The mill burned in 1907. The barn overlooks Mercer's Ford Covered Bridge (c 1880) today. Apple Grove barn was built in 1820 as part of Green Valley Farm, between Unionville and Coatesville. More about Chris Schultz on page 70.

Holiday Cutter

CHRISTOPHER SCHULTZ

CHRISTOPHER SCHULTZ uses bucolic setting of his own Birmingham Meadows Farm along Rt. 926 as inspiration for his brush. Farm house was built about 1760.

Christopher Schultz could write a book called <u>Turns in the Road</u> or <u>The Joy of Diversity</u> or <u>Do I have Enough Time For All Of This</u>?

That's the way it is with this American Realist painter who lives in a 240-year-old house with his wife, Sharon, and son, Spencer Christian, 2, exactly two miles from Andrew Wyeth's estate.

"I'd like to visit with him one of these days," said Christopher, but between his cross country running (he's qualified for the 1999 Boston Marathon); his continuous house reconstruction; his painting; his sheep shearing; and the marketing of his art, he might get it in.

Marketing is always on any Chester County artist's mind. "There is a formidable amount of talent (and competition) in the area," declared Chris, "and not just local, but of national consequence."

Chris has been painting for 20 years. After Conestoga High School, he enrolled at the Philadelphia College of Textiles and Science to study business, but dropped out. "I was searching for identity," he said. "One day I decided to go for art.

"I did a couple of drawings and made application to Hussian School of Art. They told me I needed a portfolio. I didn't know what a portfolio was.

"In a year I moved over to the Philadelphia School of Fine Art. Arthur deCosta inspired and taught me oil, acrylic, watercolor, egg tempera, different mediums. I studied under him for four years."

Chris also studied at the Uffizi in Florence and the Vatican Museum in Rome. He became a leading designer of fine porcelain for domestic and foreign markets. His work is in the White House.

He worked extensively with the Franklin Mint.

One of his greatest honors was a personal invitation to collaborate on a program with the Imperial Palace Museum in Beijing, China.

18TH CENTURY SPRING HOUSE stirs the artistic juices of "American realist" Christopher Schultz at his Birmingham Meadows Farm.

LIFE IMITATES Chris' art at Pine Creek Mills, Chester Springs, as Ben, 10-month old miniature horse, hangs out with Turk, 34-year old pony. Portrait titles are <u>BLUE WAGON</u>, top left and <u>CHET'S PONY</u>, left.

SANDRA SEVERSON

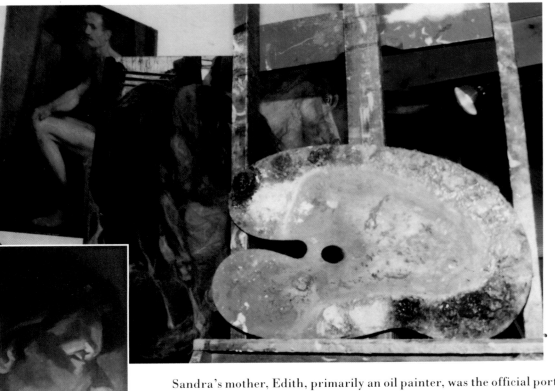

SANDRA SEVERSON'S artistic talents came directly from her mother and father, both 85 today and still painting.

But the Honeybrook resident with the penchant and extreme talent for painting horses – among a wide repertoire – spent her teenage years as a professional Philadelphia actress, soured on the lifestyle and flew to India to live in a monastery for lay people.

When she came back to Philadelphia, and then to Honeybrook to take over her late aunt's property, she brought with her the skills taught by her parents.

Her father, Gerardo Belfiore — who taught her every medium – was a print-maker and animator before Walt Disney.

Sandra's mother, Edith, primarily an oil painter, was the official portrait artist for the Archdiocese of Philadelphia. She painted priests and monsignors.

80 percent of Sandra's work consists of commissioned portraits. Her oils are Windsor Newton from England.

Keeping the line of family artists going is Kristin, 24, who is attending the Tyler Art School. "She is very talented," says mom.

SCENES AND PORTRAITS from Sandra's barn-studio in Honeybrook.

CHESTER SPRINGS home of podiatrist Dr. Herb Abbott and wife Claudia is resplendent in Chester County field stone- both outside and dramatically inside the expansive entrance foyer which is particularly well suited for entertaining with its lacquered brick flooring and dimmer lights between the wood beamed ceiling.

EQUESTRIAN ARTIST Sandra Severson explains the crafting of her painting displayed on the field stone wall of this lovely Chester Springs Road home owned by Dr. Herbert and Claudia Abbott. "I first saw the painting at the Yellow Springs Show," recalled Claudia (white slacks). "I fell completely in love with it. Herb did not seem interested in it at all. A few minutes went by and a lady put a red sticker on it. I was so disappointed. Friends came over and said how sorry they were,. . . We all went to dinner. And Herb says 'Happy Birthday' and pulls out the sales ticket."

JAMES DAVID SLOANE

James David Sloane is a gentle soul with a powerful talent.

Like so many successful artists from Chester County, this Berwyn resident's style is finely detailed realism, often with a historical twist.

The soft spoken Sloane came by his talent naturally, through his now retired artist father, Bart Phillips Sloane.

Working in the spontaneity of water color, in the tradition of his father, or the versatility of acrylic, James' careful attention is given to subtle details.

Not so subtle is the perceived tediousness in painting all of those leaves in the front of the barn at the Radnor Hunt (below). Or all of those cobblestones inside the barn (above). Sloane imitates his art at right.

James, 38, studied at Hussian School of Art, Philadelphia, and after some years involved in commercial art, pursued his interest in painting.

His limited edition prints normally sell out quickly, but can be found in many Philadelphia area galleries.

His bicycling and hiking often take him to the next focus of his sketch pad.

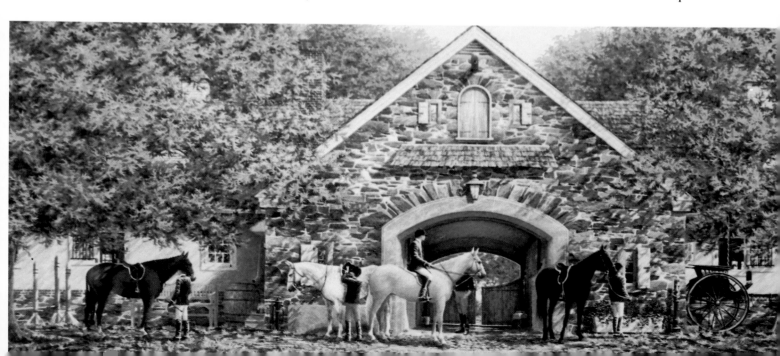

RADNOR HUNT COUNTRY- History and equestrian sport come together on Providence Road (above), at the storied Radnor Hunt Club where the Radnor Races in the spring and Radnor Hunt in October attract steeplechase riders, fancy carriages, antique cars and ultra fancy dress. Around the corner (below) sits the old blacksmith shop constructed more than two centuries ago in Whitehorse, the crossroads of Providence and Goshen Roads in Willistown Township.

THE EVER CHANGING FOCUS of West Chester artist John Suplee is evident in the home gallery scene (right photo). The symbolic landscape at left is entitled <u>LAND OF THE GIANTS</u>, meaning Howard Pyle (where he taught N.C. Wyeth), Lafayette (his headquarters) and the famous giant sycamore tree. The painting at right (partially shown) is called <u>DANCING THE ANCIENT DANCE</u>. It was inspired by his work with cows and cave walls. The figures are called petroglyphs. John suggested this would make a great headboard for a king size bed in a modern home.

• • •

ROOF TOP SCENE (left), complete with telephone poles and wires, and other neighborhood architecture (below) are a favorite subject of Suplee. So are beach scenes embellished by graceful females (two bottom photos). These American impressionistic paintings were inspired by visits to the seven-mile beach from Stone Harbor to Sea Isle City, N.J.

• • •

JOHN in his garden behind the house he shares with wife, Carol.

JOHN SUPLEE

Circumstances and people factor heavily into the development of a successful professional artist.

When John Suplee was 7, Alda Knowles, "my second mother of Copeland School Road," gave him oil painting lessons.

"We lived there outside West Chester," noted Suplee. "I always lived in old houses. My dad remodeled them."

And so it was in 1993 that Carol and John Suplee purchased an old home at the corner of Wayne and West Miner in West Chester. "The Everharts built this block in 1946," he said.

It was a perfect home for a gallery, a studio and home.

In between childhood and the present, Suplee, now 50, acquired hundreds of books by and about the masters. "If you want to get inside my brain come into this room," he said, pointing to the crammed bookcases in the bedroom.

An 18-month stay in Vienna, Austria; several years in central New York state ("some of that landscape is in my brain"); several private teachers, Japanese wood block prints that inspired painters from Van Gogh to Toulouse Letrec – all of this influenced Suplee.

But, perhaps not as much as Matisse and his freely interpreted female figures.

Suplee has done about 50 solo shows and 10 of those in recent years at the Sunset Hill Gallery, West Chester. He described the local shows as "very productive."

PLAYING THE FIELD

"I wanted to be a fine artist, but I had no idea of how to get there," declared Dane Tilghman, who went from Conestoga High to Kutztown State for an education in graphic arts he did not want. "So I bought supplies to paint and painted on the side. My first show was at the Devon Manor Nursing Home, Devon, Pa. I said to myself, 'These 80 year olds won't remember who I am but here I am. It's a show!'" That was the beginning.

OPENING DAY- check the tire mark.

Tilghman's first major show was at the Merrill Collection in West Chester in 1986 . . . 15 pieces of art, mostly pencil work. "I netted $3,000 and was a happy camper," he said. The 6-2 artist sold his "art collector oriented" work at 20 outdoor festivals between April and October. He was one of the first artists to show for corporate blacks at The Black Enterprise Golf and Tennis Challenge . . . His work appears on bank checks, 75 greeting cards, mugs . . . QVC sold 155 sets of six prints per set Feb. 1998. The same month his work appeared in Sports Illustrated.

TILGHMAN

HANGING THE MOON - No, it's not Michael Jordan.

"I used to do landscapes just to say to myself I could paint them as well as any Chester County artist," said Tilghman, 41. "But then I went into something that was more fun--painting people, with zingers. Get 'em laughing. You can say I set myself apart," said the Lionville resident.

FARMER'S GOLF

REFECTION of window in the ancient summer kitchen of the Big Bend plays on Frolic's painting of the Brandywine.

GEORGE A. (FROLIC) WEYMOUTH

CASCADE of roses and hollyhocks seems to temporarily entrance Frolic Weymouth in his vast garden at Big Bend. Below, where Frolic works, the Brandywine Museum.

FROLIC frolics at a g Bend carriage pic- (far left). His most ent painting (left) of old lady.

Inside an open air chapel on the grounds of Big Bend in Chadds Ford is this inscription on a plaque: "This chapel was built to thank God for a wonderful life, filled with fun, humor, work, sport and beauty; a close, loving family, loyal and unique friends, and a fabulous son, Mac."

It is signed by George A. Weymouth, 1995, owner of the vast, rolling estate known as Big Bend because of the direction of the Brandywine going through it.

It is a poignant description of a diverse life which includes coaching championships at the Devon Horse show; seven-goal polo player; environmentalist, horticulturist, preservationist, chairman of the Brandywine Conservancy and superb artist.

Frolic painted since early childhood, encouraged by his mother, a gifted painter in her own right. He sold his first paintings at age 8. He studied with Kleber Hall – who believed art students should develop their technical skills first – and at Yale.

He is known for his portraits in egg tempera, and his landscapes. He was one of the artists selected by NASA to paint at Cape Kennedy during the Moon Shots.

He was appointed by President Nixon to the Commission of Fine Arts and served from 1972-1977. In 1990, he received the National Art Club's annual award.

The Brandywine River Museum, operated by Weymouth's Conservancy, exhibits three generations of the Wyeth family, American still life painting and illustration. Its collections include work by hundreds of artists spanning two centuries.

HOWARD PYLE LEGACY LIVES ON

Painter's Folly (upper right), named after the man who built the house in 1856-57, lies on a hill overlooking Rt. 1 in Chadds Ford. It is famous as the place where Howard Pyle taught N.C. Wyeth how to paint. N.C.'s famous son, Andrew, now 81, uses a third floor room as a studio. But more importantly, he has a sanctuary in the friendship of Helen and George Sipala, the current owners – and occasional models for the master painter.

• • •

George and Helen (above) hold a framed Los Angeles Times book review featuring a Wyeth painting called <u>Marriage</u>. It's them. "Andy caught us by surprise," recalled Helen. "Then he had us pose for him." Upper left, Helen models for Andy as a Sisters of Charity nun. The three paintings were done in the widow's walk above Andy's studio.

A portrait of Helga Testorf adorns the green wall in the family room.

Below left, Helen is painted again by Wyeth in <u>Beauty Rest</u>. "He likes to paint in blacks and whites," she said. "But there is no rhyme or reason to what he paints."

On the right is the living room and a series of Wyeths leading up the staircase to a Lincoln by Kennett Square artist Rea Redifer.

HOUSES
AND
STUDIOS

OF
FAMOUS
PAINTERS

PROCEEDS from N.C. Wyeth's Treasure Island series of 17 paintings enabled patriarch of America's first family of art to build his studio (left) and home (below) in 1911. Brandywine Conservancy maintains studio in immaculate condition and offers guided tours by appointment. Carolyn, N.C.'s second daughter, held art classes there for decades. Andrew occasionally paints there today. House and studio (front and rear) are on a hill about 1 mile behind Brandywine Museum. In 1997, the two structures were declared National Historic landmarks by the National Park Service.

ANDREW WYETH'S main studio (top) is located on Rt. 100 south about one-half mile in back of the Brandywine Museum grounds. The renown son of N.C. also paints in a separate studio on an estate (left) along the Brandywine he shares with wife, Betsy, located on Rt. 100 North about one-mile from Rt. 1. A fourth Wyeth studio is on the third floor of Painter's Folly, the old Howard Pyle studio, on Route 1. Above, the remains of the Avondale studio and home of Thomas Eakins, one of America's great painters in the mid-1800's.

CHESHIRE HUNT UNIONVILLE, PA.

THANKSGIVING DAY 1997

AUTUMN

TRANQUILITY of a lone hunter's route - from donkey business (above), through the glorious umbrella of autumn's color and the fading light going home- in Pickering Hunt country, Chester Springs.

IN THE HEART of downtown Oxford in the southwestern end of Chester County is the restored Oxford Hotel, circa 1890 (now apartments) where it is not uncommon to view an Amish buggy passing by. Indeed, this IS Amish country, as witness the clutch of boys just off the school bus on a nearby country road.

THE HEADLINE ABOVE in the form of a sign at the head of the driveway is a figment of Howard Buzzard's self-deprecating sense of humor. The Roost is, in fact, where Howard and Lucy Buzzard enjoy 24 acres of equestrian heaven just one-half mile from the Yellow Springs Inn that Gen. Washington used as a hospital during the Revolutionary War. The property was in disrepair when Howard bought it 27 years ago.

THE 1936 MERCEDES ROADSTER points down a driveway that extends 400 yards to Art School Road. Behind the roadster is a house (upper right) whose main section was built about 1820. When Howard bought the property in 1971 each floor of the main house was "filled halfway to the ceiling with empty liquor bottles. The barn had been burned to the ground." The fireplace, circa 1780, was part of the summer kitchen. It adjoins the indoor pool which was built in 1992.

PALADIUM WINDOW at one end of the pool exposes a double decker spring house (c 1800) with real spring water running through the cellar. Howard and Lucy wave from the 1934 Rolls Royce alongside a barn that can board 10 horses and contains five antique carriages from a time when the real estate developer was involved in coaching. Howard and Lucy are both involved in raising funds for Yellow Springs charity events.

THE BLIZZARD OF 1996
WEST CHESTER, PA.

WINTER

18-22 WEST GAY STREET THE BAR

THE RESTAURANT & THE BAR

THE BLIZZARD OF 1996 yielded snow mountains in downtown West Chester: La Cocotte Restaurant (top left) and The Bar and Restaurant (top right) on Gay St., Jane Chalfant dress shop (left) on High St., and home of late artist Howard Thorne, 27 E. Union St. (right).

A LONGWOOD GARDENS CHRISTMAS

MAGIC OF CHRISTMAS 1997 is reflected in these scenes from Longwood Gardens (left and above) and the Brandywine Museum (below and right). At Brandywine, young lady examines painting in the Andrew Wyeth room; rare Victorian doll house is on display as well as tree and wreath decorations made by volunteers from natural materials found in woods and streams. At Longwood, a statuesque great blue heron overlooks colorfully bordered pond in the conservatory; Santa Claus stands sculpted from a 54' diameter white oak; lighted reindeer cavort on the conservatory lawn and a sunset contrasts with the tree lights.

A Brandyw

Christmas

THE DEEPEST Chester County snow in 38 years, the aftermath of a virtual blizzard, had its opportunistic moments, like a chance to take the wraps off the antique sleigh, tack up the horses and head for the open country. And so it was on Sunday, January 7, 1996 that this scene right out of a Currier and Ives painting took place at H. Richard Dietrich Jr.'s Bryn Coed Farm in Chester Springs, Pa. Dietrich ran a tractor through his farm roads to batten down the three feet of snow before the sleigh full of revelers attempted the run.

The End

Southern Chester County

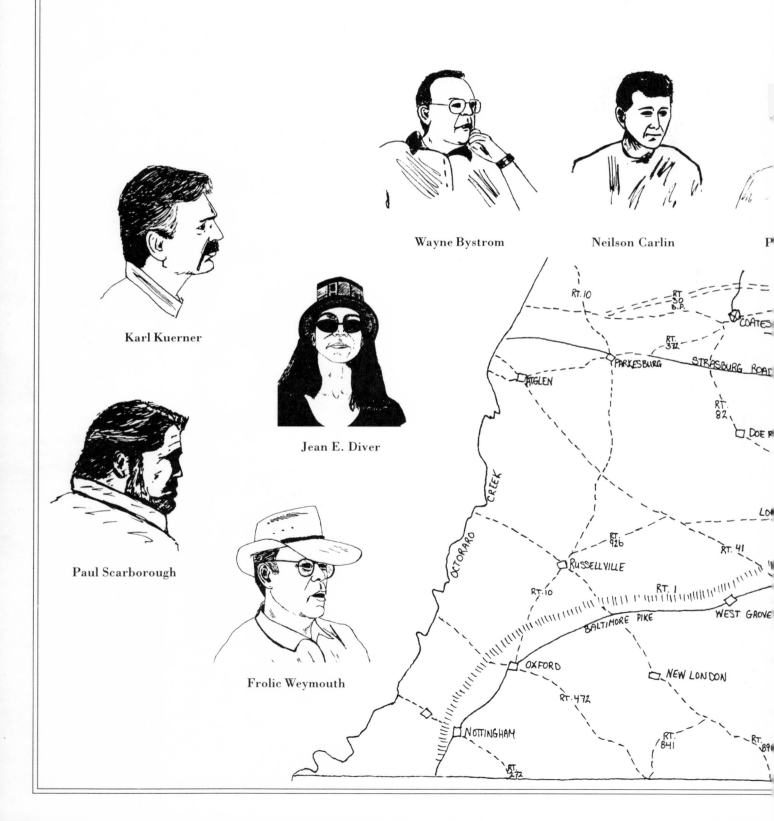

Wayne Bystrom

Neilson Carlin

Karl Kuerner

Jean E. Diver

Paul Scarborough

Frolic Weymouth